J 629.225 Bow
Bowman, Chris, 1990-
Fire trucks /
$24.95   ocn954719919

W9-AMO-656

3 4028 09229 0254
HARRIS COUNTY PUBLIC LIBRARY

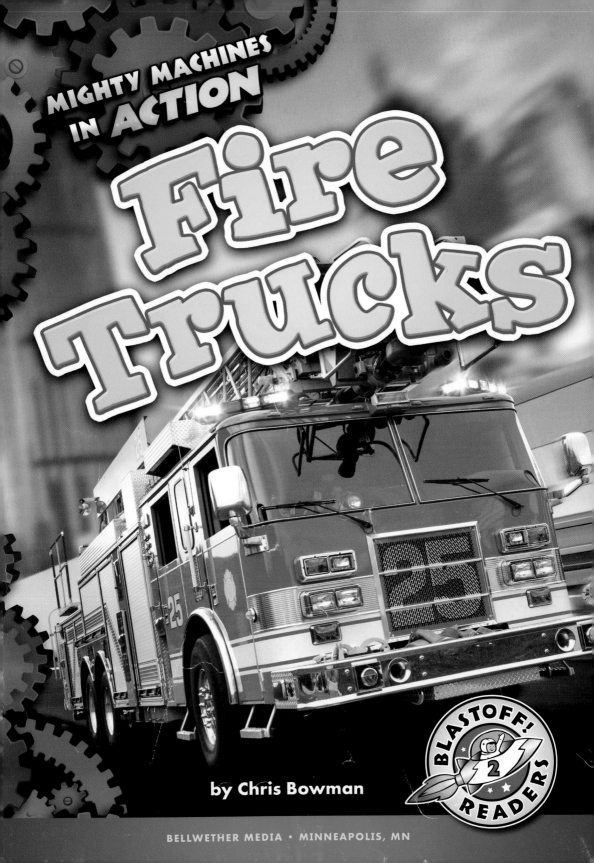

MIGHTY MACHINES IN ACTION

Fire Trucks

by Chris Bowman

BELLWETHER MEDIA · MINNEAPOLIS, MN

BLASTOFF! READERS

2

Note to Librarians, Teachers, and Parents:

Blastoff! Readers are carefully developed by literacy experts and combine standards-based content with developmentally appropriate text.

Level 1 provides the most support through repetition of high-frequency words, light text, predictable sentence patterns, and strong visual support.

Level 2 offers early readers a bit more challenge through varied simple sentences, increased text load, and less repetition of high-frequency words.

Level 3 advances early-fluent readers toward fluency through increased text and concept load, less reliance on visuals, longer sentences, and more literary language.

Level 4 builds reading stamina by providing more text per page, increased use of punctuation, greater variation in sentence patterns, and increasingly challenging vocabulary.

Level 5 encourages children to move from "learning to read" to "reading to learn" by providing even more text, varied writing styles, and less familiar topics.

Whichever book is right for your reader, Blastoff! Readers are the perfect books to build confidence and encourage a love of reading that will last a lifetime!

This edition first published in 2017 by Bellwether Media, Inc.

No part of this publication may be reproduced in whole or in part without written permission of the publisher. For information regarding permission, write to Bellwether Media, Inc., Attention: Permissions Department, 5357 Penn Avenue South, Minneapolis, MN 55419.

Library of Congress Cataloging-in-Publication Data

Names: Bowman, Chris, 1990- author.
Title: Fire Trucks / by Chris Bowman.
Description: Minneapolis, MN : Bellwether Media, Inc., 2017. | Series:
    Blastoff! Readers. Mighty Machines in Action | Audience: Ages 5-8. |
    Audience: K to grade 3. | Includes bibliographical references and index.
Identifiers: LCCN 2016033334 (print) | LCCN 2016035422 (ebook) | ISBN
    9781626176041 (hardcover : alk. paper) | ISBN 9781681033341 (ebook)
Subjects: LCSH: Fire engines–Juvenile literature.
Classification: LCC TH9372 .B69 2017 (print) | LCC TH9372 (ebook) | DDC
    629.225–dc23
LC record available at https://lccn.loc.gov/2016033334

Text copyright © 2017 by Bellwether Media, Inc. BLASTOFF! READERS and associated logos are trademarks and/or registered trademarks of Bellwether Media, Inc. SCHOLASTIC, CHILDREN'S PRESS, and associated logos are trademarks and/or registered trademarks of Scholastic Inc.

Editor: Christina Leighton   Designer: Jon Eppard

Printed in the United States of America, North Mankato, MN.

Table of **Contents**

GETTING THE CALL

A call comes in to the fire station. A building is on fire!

Firefighters rush to prepare.
They all jump in the fire truck.

The truck's lights flash and the **siren** screams. The fire truck speeds away.

It arrives at the
building in no time.
Then it helps put
out the fire!

FIGHTING FIRE

Fire trucks are used during **emergencies**. They carry firefighters and their gear.

They are often
found in cities
and towns.

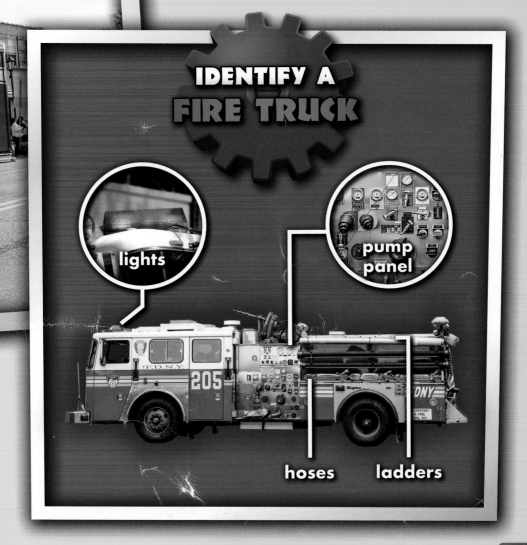

IDENTIFY A
FIRE TRUCK

lights

pump
panel

hoses   ladders

Small fire trucks
work on mountains.
They drive over
rough ground.

Larger fire trucks work at airports.
They put out airplane fires.

LADDERS, HOSES, AND TOOLS

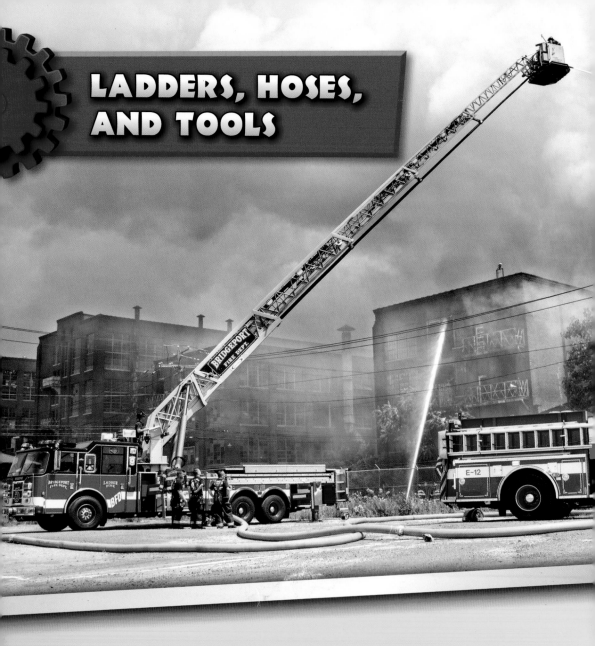

Many fire trucks have ladders and **cherry pickers**. These help firefighters reach tall buildings.

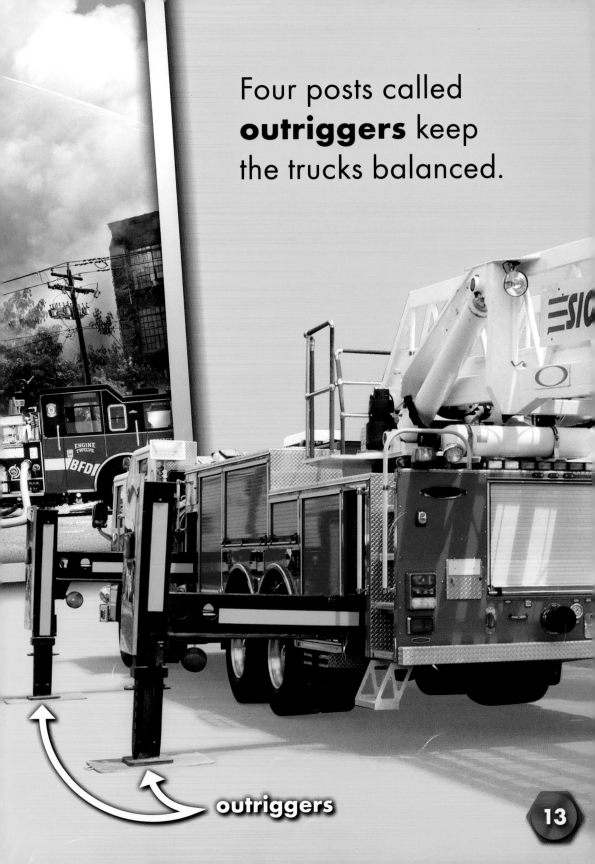

Four posts called **outriggers** keep the trucks balanced.

outriggers

Fire trucks with hoses connect to **standpipes** and **fire hydrants**. A truck's **pump panel** controls the flow of water.

pump panel →

fire hydrant →

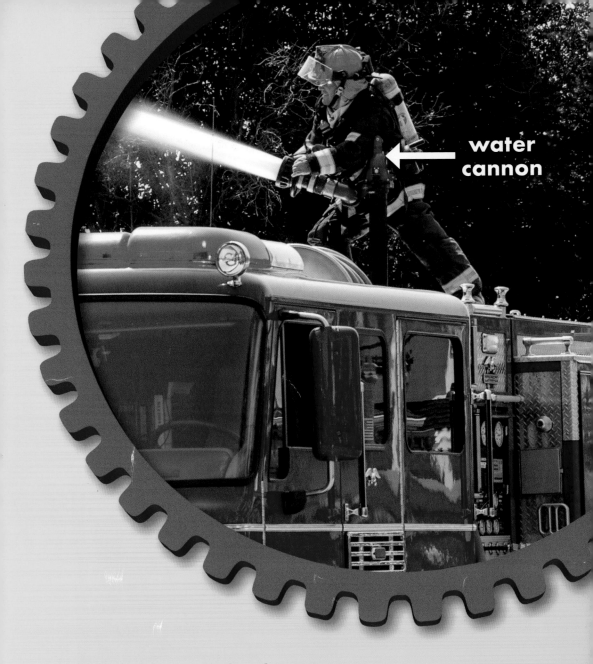

water
cannon

Some trucks have **water cannons**. They spray water right from the truck!

Eight people fit in the truck's **cab**. Two sit in the front seat.

BIG JOB BIG MACHINE

HD-57 Aerial Ladder

height: 11 feet (3.4 meters)

average human

length: 35 feet (10.7 meters)

jump seat

The others sit on the **jump seat** behind them.

The trucks store a lot of gear.
They carry helmets, masks,
and air tanks.

Cutting tools and axes help firefighters enter places with speed.

MACHINE PROFILE
QUINT FIRE TRUCK

A quint does the work of two trucks. It has everything firefighters need!

1) pump panel
2) water tank
3) hoses
4) aerial device
5) ground ladders

Fire trucks move fast to catch fires. They have what firefighters need to get the job done.

These powerful machines help keep us safe!

Glossary

cab—the part of the fire truck where the firefighters sit

cherry pickers—platforms that can be raised to help firefighters work in high places

emergencies—serious and dangerous events that need quick attention

fire hydrants—short metal pipes found outdoors that connect to water lines

jump seat—the back seat of the fire truck

outriggers—metal poles that stick out of the fire truck to balance it when the ladder is used

pump panel—the part of the fire truck that controls water flow through the hoses

siren—an alarm that makes a loud sound to warn of danger

standpipes—long metal pipes found in buildings that connect to water lines

water cannons—tools that shoot water at high speeds

To Learn More

AT THE LIBRARY

Carr, Aaron. *Fire Trucks*. New York, N.Y.: AV2 by Weigl, 2016.

Fortuna, Lois. *Fire Trucks*. New York, N.Y.: Gareth Stevens Publishing, 2016.

Graubart, Norman D. *Fire Trucks*. New York, N.Y.: PowerKids Press, 2015.

ON THE WEB

Learning more about fire trucks is as easy as 1, 2, 3.

1. Go to www.factsurfer.com.

2. Enter "fire trucks" into the search box.

3. Click the "Surf" button and you will see a list of related web sites.

With factsurfer.com, finding more information is just a click away.

Index

The images in this book are reproduced through the courtesy of: ryasick, front cover; Corbis/ VCG/ Getty Images, p. 4; Nick Starichenko, p. 5; Associated Press, pp. 6-7; Mike Brake, pp. 7, 15; Barry Blackburn, pp. 8-9; jiawangkun, p. 9 (top left); Leonard Zhukovsky, p. 9 (top right, bottom); Steve Photography, p. 10; Sorin Alb, pp. 10-11; Keith Muratori, pp. 12-13; Jim Parkin, p. 13; Pete Titmuss/ Alamy, p. 14; MBI/ Alamy, pp. 16-17; mario loiselle, pp. 18-19; Joedamadman, p. 19; blurAZ, pp. 20-21.

Harris County Public Library, Houston, TX